D0687089

Above: How Mrs. Athanasios spots the liars in the market.
Clockwise from left. 1. Overly smooth or silken speech; 2. Unbroken or hypnotic eye contact;
3. Hand gestures over mouth or touching nose; 4. Inappropriate or invasive body contact;
5. Too good to be true.

Copyright © 2008 by Steven Saunders

All rights reserved. No part of this book may be used or reproduced
in any manner whatsoever without written permission from the
publisher except in the case of brief quotations embodied in critical
articles or reviews. For information address Walker & Company,
175 Fifth Avenue, New York, New York 10010.

Published by
Walker Publishing Company, Inc., New York

Printed on recycled paper.

Library of Congress Cataloging-in-Publication Data
has been applied for.

ISBN-10: 0-8027-1680-6
ISBN-13: 978-0-8027-1680-4

Visit Walker & Company's Web site
at www.walkerbooks.com

First U.S. edition 2008

1 3 5 7 9 10 8 6 4 2

Designed and typeset by
Wooden Books Ltd, Glastonbury, UK

Printed in the United States of America

MIND TRICKS
ANCIENT AND MODERN

Steven Saunders

with illustrations by Matt Tweed

Walker & Company
New York

This book is dedicated to children worldwide,
and especially Anthony, Ellie, Freddy, Heather and Ivan—my teachers all.

Immense gratitude to John Martineau for his editing and support and Matt Tweed for his illustrations.
Eternal thanks and love for being in my life to Josie, Blossie, Douglas, Isy, Louisa, Al, George and Judy,
Maggie, Stu, John, Judith, Pete, Matt Zepler, Chris Gilham, Peter East, Charles Baker, Ursula Scrizzi,
Eileen Watkin Seymour, Clive Digby-Jones and David Grove.

All deference and credit to the modern masters Richard Bandler and John Grinder, Eric Berne, Carl G.
Jung, Sigmund Freud, G. I. Gurdjieff, John Bolby, and the many ancient Masters.

Thanks to Isaac Asimov for Psychohistory and the laws of robotics.

Above: A "swish", or replacement of one mental image with another.
Here Mr. Dixit erases his negative self-image by means of a simple neolithic device still
available today and free to anyone with a vivid imagination and a spare minute or two.

CONTENTS

INTRODUCTION

Welcome to this small compendium of the tools and tricks of the mind trade, a trade as old as the roots of civilization itself.

What is a mind trick? Well, a famous old one was King Solomon's judgment on two women bringing a baby before him, both claiming it was theirs. "Cut it in half!" he said, which prompted one of them to beg him to give the baby to the other, thus giving herself away as the true mother of the baby. Solomon's shock-trick brought out the unconscious motivations of the actors. This is also a feature of tricking minds with hypnosis—distracting the conscious mind while operating on the unconscious.

The Vikings were renowned for trickery in battle, their favorite being feigned flight, causing opponents to break formation and so become vulnerable to a counterattack. In ancient warfare the side that best held formation would normally win, so running away and then ambushing those chasing was a feature of many battles. Children, too, naturally discover the fun of this game.

Modern mind tricks take both useful and sinister forms, whether embedded commands in advertisments, feats of mind reading, or phobia cures. In *Star Wars* a Jedi hand-gesture accompanied by "these are not the droids you are looking for" works its magic.

Everyone, unconsciously, uses mind tricks on other people all the time—presidents, aides, shamans, seductresses, and children, as well as the professional tricksters who call themselves magicians.

Try out the tricks in this book on yourself and your friends. They are fun, practical, and, done properly, can occasionally change someone's life, as indeed they have done for centuries.

GETTING OUT OF YOUR BOX
cosmologies and the worlds we all inhabit

In the earliest story known to man, Gilgamesh, king of Uruk, weakened at home, makes an epic journey, exploring distant lands and confronting adversaries, both inner and outer. In the same way we all have to grow up, leave home, and transcend the ego.

Human beings are pattern-forming animals, and upbringings and lifestyles can often act as familiar prisons. There are, however, some useful mind tricks that can crack open these boxes.

A start is to question the hidden and multivarious assumptions that often underlie human patterns. Learn to ask yourself what you assume to be true about yourself, the world, and others, and make a point of spotting other people's assumptions.

To help with this, use the "Why?" trick, a simple question that helps break hidden assumptions. Young children go through a phase of asking it, so try seeing the world through a child's eyes. Find something that bothers you and repeatedly ask "Why?" of yourself until the answers get deeper. Then, when you get somewhere and want to find out how to implement this in your life try using the simple related trick of repeatedly asking yourself "How?"

Languages, like national myths or religions, are further boxes people grow up in, affecting the way the world is perceived. Learning a new language is a great mind-expanding trick, and bilingual children are known to have higher IQs. Many misunderstandings are simply caused by people having different personal mappings of words even in the same language!

Experience object-oriented English another way by using phrases like *As you are experiencing your moving, what knowing is emerging?*

Above: Boxes: In your approach to life, the universe and everything, are you mostly science-, faith- or philosophy-biased? Now imagine you are in a box with your label on it. Close your eyes and imagine who else is in there with you. What kind of things can you talk about? Now imagine swapping places with someone else in another box. What are the people there like? Imagine there is a box outside the boxes; can you get outside that one and look back in? What else is going on around you out there? What other kind of labels can you play with?

Above: Personality stereotypes can be difficult boxes to get out of. Various mind tricks have evolved over the centuries to help with this process, perhaps the best of which is the human capacity for modeling, or theatre. Dressing up as a sporting-type will not make you fit, but it will give you some insights into fitness. Acting a mathematician on stage will not make you good at math, but it might help you understand the kinds of issues that occupy mathematicians' minds. Use your imagination and natural acting abilities to move between stereotypical boxes and get out of your own.

LISTEN TO MY VOICE
hypnosis, sleep and other strange states of mind

Hypnos was the Greek god of sleep, and many early civilizations used the dream state for healing and personal revelation. While sleeping in a temple or grotto, the gods would visit bringing an important dream, food for the psyche that many modern psychotherapists still use today. In hypnosis, a trance-like state similar to sleep, the hypnotist replaces the gods and makes suggestions to the subject.

To hypnotize someone, talk to their subconscious without their conscious mind being aware of what you are doing. Do this by adding subtle song into your speech, using embedded commands like "notice your arm relaxing" or "don't fall asleep," building safe rapport, and creating gentle shifts in focus. Once hypnotized, people are free from their conscious minds and able to access unconscious information and expression. Contrary to the claims of stage magicians they always have complete control of themselves.

Self-hypnosis is another mind trick which can be useful. A simple yoga practice involves lying down, making yourself warm and comfortable, and then successively tensing and relaxing your legs, then arms, torso, neck, head, toes, thoughts and so on, before adding an affirmation like "I am simply the best!"

Or you might want to try lucid dreaming, where you wake up inside your dream, and can then completely direct and control it. To do this trick, think of your dreams in the day time while wondering if you are dreaming at the same time. Look at your hands and say to yourself "Next time I am dreaming I will look at my hands and remember I am dreaming." To do it with someone else, agree to meet them in your dreams at a certain place and time.

Above: Brenda is too entranced in her mind and projections. Her inner world constrains what she can perceive of the outer world. The trick is to realize that everything she perceives is only telling her about herself. Learn from your mistakes, and let others do the same. Sometimes you have to trip over the exit (here a rabbit).

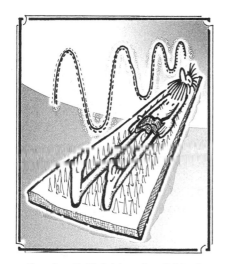

Above: Swami Satish, fresh from a fire walk (where he visualized cool wet grass), overcomes his next painful exercise by focusing inside his body, rather than on his skin.

Above: Clitus relaxes in the Abaton (dream room) of an ancient Greek Asclepieion (sleep temple). Cassandra mediates so the Gods can slip their message into his dreams.

WHAT DOES IT MEAN?
glyph tricks and symbolic functions

Symbols are visual mind tricks that have been used for millennia and still surround us today as cleverly designed logos and signs. Early symbols on clay tablets, originally used to record grave goods in Crete and Egypt, migrated to letters to form alphabets as a standard for communicating information. For example the letter "A" evolved from the sacred cow of the pre-Egyptian nomadic tribes (*below*), and "G" and "D" come from "stick" (hit/strike/knock) and "door" respectively, so "God" means "knock on door" (*see Matthew 7.7*). A symbol thus accesses deep cultural wisdom alongside its natural powers. Love-hearts, pentacles, and crosses all have deep meanings that are intuitively grasped by the subconscious and are further enriched as the conscious mind understands them better. Symbols are widely used in mind tricks as objects of meditation or worn as talismans for healing or manifestation.

The Tarot is a more complex set of symbols. Derived from ancient Egyptian sources, they represent the hero's journey, similar to the twelve labors of Hercules, or the signs of the zodiac. Ensuring you understand archetypes like these can promote insight into yourself and others, so research, meditate upon, and try acting out different symbols, a useful trick if you are a writer creating characters and their journeys for a screenplay or novel.

Numbers have always had strong symbolic qualities too. Two is company, three is a crowd. What is your lucky number? Why?

Above: Symbols. A sign of the times; Penelope and Donald choose the "Smiley" for today's group meditation. They first research the earliest meanings and interpretations of the symbol. Next they pause, slow down, and stop thinking, using the pause between their breaths to find their inner stillness. They then bring the symbol in to mind.

Above: Picking a Tarot card, like throwing runes, using the I Ching, or scrying tea leaves, uses the fact that the inner world is reflected in the outer world to present consciousness with messages that may be acceptable. The spread above might indicate a destruction of the egoic mind by a self-revelation (The Tower), followed by a phase of innocent bliss (The Fool), leading to the development of intuitive powers (The High Priestess), and alignment to destiny (The Lovers).

THE STORY OF A LIFE
metaphor tricks and drive-thru symbols

Metaphors (from Greek *metaphora*) are close relatives of symbols that use analogies to efficiently enrich meaning. We use them all the time ("mortgage meltdown," "hit a snag," etc) without realizing just what clever tricks they can be.

For example, if "life is a journey" (a very common metaphor) then why not dream up a truly epic voyage for yourself, or at least explore what might be around the corner? In ancient shamanic traditions people often visualized, or recited, epics of travels through woods, wildernesses and caves to experience a meaningful journey and return with the resources and materials needed for a rich and successful life. The same trick still works today. Close your eyes and imagine yourself having an adventure, or guide a friend through one (try not to impose on them any of your own words or ideas—use their own words back to them). Break through walls that have barred your way, learn to *plot a course* through life.

In the ancient Chinese science of Feng-Shui the metaphor is externalized and the internal arrangement of the home and even the landscape itself are all studied as symbolic metaphors, affecting the relative probabilities of certain outcomes for the person living in that arrangement. The *perfect spot* invokes perfect dreams and a perfect life, its journey guided by a natural balance of opposites.

Metaphors are also used in high-level mind trick manipulations of mathematical and physical equations by scientists (*see below*).

Above: A world of metaphor. Quan relaxes surrounded by a balanced landscape, inner and outer, dreaming a happy life into being.

SPEAK FRIEND AND ENTER
language spells and the doors they open

Doors open to friendly faces and words, so it pays to speak the language of the gatekeeper. As there are visual thinkers ("I see what you mean"), auditory communicators ("sounds right") and people who are more feelings-based ("in touch"), good speech-writers will use all the senses to connect with the most people they can.

Matching an audience's metaphors is a trick so powerful that it can unwittingly have its downside: "Don't look back!," for instance, contains the hidden command that eventually causes poor Orpheus to lose Eurydice. "Look straight ahead!" works better.

To maximize the power of language trickery use extra clean questions (*see opposite*), that minimally intrude your own words on the reality of the other person. As in hypnosis, this enables them to give full expression to their own thoughts in their own terms, solving things for themselves. Try and keep a silent mind and emotional stillness, remaining unattached to the answers.

If someone is not feeling heard, then give them their words back, perfectly repeated, or give lots of affirming "um-hums," "yeps" and "oks" as they talk. If you want to interrupt, take a deep breath and count to ten this works anytime something rash might otherwise emerge! Another trick to get great results with your speech is to use your whole body to send your message, from stomach to nose. Good orators separate their words, round off their edges (*see below*) and time the interval between key points to fit the thinking cycle of their audience (*lower opposite*).

And do you have a sense of ... ?
And whereabouts could that be?

And does that have a size or shape or form?
And what kind of edge or boundary could that have?

And what could be just around that?
And how far does that go?

Continue asking the above questions until you find the source. Or start outside and work inwards!

Left: Using clean questions to unravel a problem held in the body. Clean questions contain no references to anything that might intrude.

Some examples to discover sources: "And where could that have come from?" "And what kind of you were you before you became this/that you?" "And what happens just before?"

Ontological clean questions: "And what do you know about that?" "And what does that know?" "And how old could that be?"

Creative and Contextual questions: "And now/then what can happen?" "And then what happens?" "And is there anything else about that?" "And is there a relationship between ...?"

Refining and Metaphorical questions: "And is there anything else?" "And that's like what?" "And what kind of that could that be?"

Above: Sigabbar interrogates a rival Assyrian mage about the new cult of Marduk. The secret of his legendary success is not torture, but a clever trick. He carefully notices when his prisoner relaxes or stops thinking and chooses those moments to ask his next question, thus keeping the flow of thoughts running and revealing the hidden knowledge within. Practice this on your friends and enemies alike, using modern biofeedback machines.

REFRAMING
tricks to see things in other ways

One of the oldest mind tricks, and still one of the best, involves changing the point of view to shift the perception of a situation. For example, the parable of the prodigal son reframes common fairness as unconditional love, and fairy tales or scientific breakthroughs often reframe family or social patterns in such a way that they can be overcome (*top row opposite*). Humor is also fundamentally based upon reframing, satire upon exaggeration, using changed contexts (*middle row opposite*) and counter-examples (*bottom row opposite*) to make the target ridiculous. Salespeople use this trick, e.g., saying "picture yourself in these, the envy of all!" reframing clothes in envy, or asking questions that are framed to force certain responses. Caesar shifts frames to one in which his policy seems good and fair.

Many heads are better than one, and many perspectives can aid clarity on complex projects. Dilts' Neurological Levels are six modern perspectives useful for gaining a complete understanding of a system: *Purpose* (why), *Identity* (what), *Beliefs* (assume), *Capabilities* (skill), *Behaviors* (how), and *Environment* (where/when). With Edward De Bono's thinking hats (*below*), a group rotates through roles together (*Facts and Figures, Instinctive Reaction, Critic, Optimist, Creator, Overview*) covering perspectives while avoiding contradictory dynamics. Good ideas, for example, are often killed at birth when creatives and critics coincide. Try wearing some other hats!

Above: After four days of trekking, Monsieur Montgolfier becomes anxious as he cannot see the woods for the trees.

Above: Taking to the air in his brother's balloon, he rejoices as suddenly everything becomes clear.

Above: Bertie is so horrified that his pristine pool has been defiled by a bug that he can't touch the water.

Above: Laurence, crawling through the desert sand, is so thirsty he would drink dirty dishwater.

Above: "All dogs are uncontrollable gluttons," exclaims Princess Gonerille, waving her arms in horror.

Above: Prince Henry exercises total self control, and so does his dog, disproving the Princess's claim.

Memory Tricks
learning how to learn

One of the most useful tricks anyone can learn is the art of memory, and for centuries almost exactly the same kinds of mental devices have been used by memory professionals across the world. How do they all work? By visualization and exaggeration.

For example, a widely used trick was to imagine or invent for oneself a large and familiar house (or theater in the Renaissance), and choose a standard route by which to visit the rooms. Do this for yourself, smelling each room, noticing furniture, window-ledges, and so on. Now put memory objects in each room, an airplane (tickets), a white flood (milk). Make them surreal, oversized, painted blue, bleeding, exploding, or boiling (*see opposite top*).

A great memory–game for four or more people in a car is the one where each person says, "On holiday this year I packed in my suitcase: ...," and then recites the list so far, adding one more item like "some sticky goo," "a frog," whatever. To win this game, use the trick shown (*opposite center*). Visualize each object interpenetrating the next in some way, making a mess or wrapping around.

To memorize numbers (or cards), you will need a lookup table (*lower opposite*), that turns numbers into letters that can be related to objects starting with that letter. Then just use the system above.

Dyslexia is sometimes caused by teaching children to read with a moving finger that later turns into moving words (*below left*). Better to point to each word in turn (*below right*).

14

Above: A memory house with objects for a shopping list. Starting in the library (left), a giant broken sploshing bottle reminds you to buy wine. A large dying fish flops wetly in the hall (buy fishfood). A winged envelope flutters up and down the stairs (envelopes). In the study a picture has fallen to the floor and is melting (go to the picture-framers). Make the memory objects as vivid and surreal as possible. Now look away and see if you can remember all four!

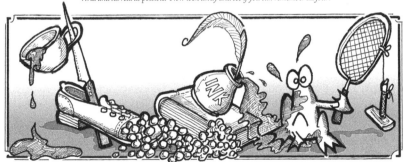

Above: A memory chain of twelve objects. Goo, Cup, Knife, Shoe, Peas, Book, Ink, Feather, Frog, Tennis Racket, String, Hammer. Start on the left and then add each object in turn. In your mind make the cup spill the goo, the knife saw through the bottom of the shoe, the ink spill on the frog's foot. The more the objects interpenetrate or strongly or pleasingly relate the more easily the chain will be remembered. With a surprisingly small amount of practice, 100 objects can be remembered in order with ease.

0 = C or D	5 = F or V	E.G., 3861 = Mud (on a) Ballgown (cut by)
1 = L, J, or W	6 = S	Scissors (attached to a) Lamp.
2 = T	7 = Y, G	
3 = M	8 = B, H, K	Or use doubles, so 3861 = 38 61 = MiKe SaiL
4 = R, P	9 = N	= A microphone painted on a sail

Above: A number key. Use words starting with these letters to remember long numbers, or develop your own key. You will need to know your key very well to make the system fluid.

CREATIVE FREEDOM
tricks to get the juices flowing

Creativity is an enigmatic commodity. In ancient times people appealed to the Muses for inspiration. Scholars would get their heart beating, pacing up and down while speaking to a slave. Charles Dickens took long brisk walks. Relaxing helps too—Archimedes famously discovered the law of displacement in his bath.

Random changes of mood like laughter, music, conversation, or location can also get original playful ideas flowering. Explore a lane, climb a hill, drink with friends, or have a snooze under a tree. Fear of mistakes destroys creative freedom so be like a child, walking along a wall without knowing it is dangerous.

Try being creative with your entire life. Ask yourself what you want to achieve in life, what you would like to have done by the end of it, or what you would like to be remembered for. Work out the key things that are necessary for your total satisfaction and decide which of them you have too much of and which need more attention. Explore your values and ask yourself how happy you are with their manifestation in your work and home. Imagine what your most creative friend might come up with.

Another great trick to break open your thinking is to ask "What if?" Many limitations on thinking are culturally- or self-imposed. For example, you may like bicycling but don't go often. Ask "Why" to discover that you get tired going up hills. But "*What if* it wasn't tiring?" "*What if* there were no hills?" The solution: move to a new flatter area, or invent the power-assisted bicycle.

Creativity works best when you are cheerful, so if you are not feeling great write a list of ten reasons why your life is fantastic.

Above: The Disney Technique. Placing different aspects of a project, Planner, Creative, and Critic, in different locations allows each their own "thinking space." Start in one role, find out what you know there, name it, then totally change spaces, and so on. It can also help to use different physical locations, and even to change clothes to suit the roles.

Above: A Releasing Spell, useful for getting rid of blocks of all kinds. This particular example is derived from the Pentateuch (first five books of the Torah), which contains prayer forms designed to release projections on other people. With hand on heart and with full intention, release all other people from your perceptions of them.

HITTING THE TARGET
secrets of success tricks

If you want to get really good at something, start young. Mozart was composing and performing short pieces of music from the age of five. Learning from mistakes also refines performance— Edison famously tried over 10,000 ways to make a light bulb before succeeding. If you can't start young then practice makes perfect. Having a great rival can also be motivating (often a younger sibling becomes the greater player as an adult). During practice, an exciting trick is to set harder targets (*opposite top*).

Underpinning success in all martial arts, sports, and leadership is stillness of mind. In the ancient martial art of Jujitsu, the first to act usually loses, so both combatants wait. Top baseball hitters and goal kickers make themselves calm and still before striking. Patterned gestures, or anchors (*below*), can assist with this.

Success also lies in simplifying what you are doing, in even the smallest things (*lower opposite*). Peak performance appears and feels effortless, so if something is hard work then try varying it slightly, one thing at a time, until it feels easier. Many top performers also mimick themselves, copying the emotional state of excellence from their specialty into other life areas. Try it for yourself!

When struggling, get clear on what you want, why, and how to get it, specifically. Do something massive that means you cannot turn back, like Julius Caesar crossing the Rubicon.

Above: Archery practice. Instead of aiming for the straw target, Robin shoots at a narrow post, a peeled willow wand, narrowing his focus. In medieval England, "laying the body into the bow" required a young and flexible body and football was outlawed from 1314 to promote compulsory archery practice. The French paid dearly at Agincourt!

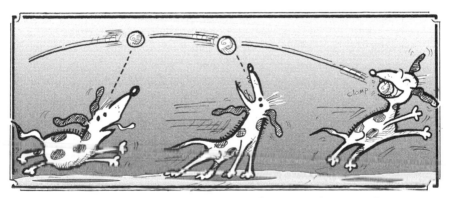

Above: By standing still, jumping, or sliding just before catching, Fido simplifies his body movement at the critical moment. Head and eye compensations for variable leg movements are reduced to zero. Moving faster than the ball slows his sense of time, allowing him to make finely tuned adjustments.

Left: Anchors. Widely used by sports and media professionals, these tricks instantly change your emotional state so you perform how you want to in the moment. To set up an anchor, first choose the state you wish to embody, then recall three different occasions when you had this desired state. In turn, visualize, feel and hear each occasion. As the feeling starts to peak, make a unique gesture (e.g., clasp your hands, touch a fingertip, or flare your nostrils). Do this three times for each occasion, using the same gesture. Repeat every day for a while. Trigger the gesture in a circumstance where it is desired.

TUNING TRICKS
empathy and body-snatching

A great life trick in all ages has been the art of seeing things from another person's perspective. Diplomats need this skill and people that can't do it tend to be short on friends. Empathy is one of the most important elements of psychological health.

Many people start empathizing by thinking: "If I were that person, how would I be feeling, what would I be thinking?," but the skill can be developed much further. In *body matching*, a person quietly copies the word and gesture patterns of someone else, following their precise body postures and motions until the movements feel easy. Once inside the "other person's skin," so to speak, feelings and even thoughts will arise that can be uncannily accurate.

Similarly, Buddhist and Hindu statues were designed as body models, objects of contemplation for living a life congruent to an ideal. In fact, congruence can be learned. Think of a few things you love and, taking each in turn, say "I love this" and notice where in your body you feel a response. This is your congruence signal. Saying the same about things you dislike will reveal your incongruence signal. Using these signals can enhance your intuition

The ancient Greek doctrine of the humors took this further, identifying each organ with an emotion; the gall bladder with envy, the liver with courage or cowardice, the guts with instinctive feelings, and so on. In the same way, there are different qualities of mental activity: reasoning, imagining, believing, meditating and wanting. A good empath, like the Oracle at Delphi, feels these differences, and can effectively mind-read. Practice the tricks you've already learned and this skill will develop naturally.

Above: In the same way that matter bends space-time, different consciousnesses act as centers of gravity, attracting one another. Imagine you can space travel from your planet to another and look out through someone else's eyes.

Above: Ptollie likes the look of Cleo. He looks into her eyes to see how she sees him. Then he looks inside that him to see the her that that him sees. Then he looks inside that her to see the him that that her sees. And so on, until ...

Above: Body matching. Nephi copies Akhe's strange walk, a few more adjustments left to master.

Above: Tuning in. Good music requires musicians be in tune. Empathize to make good vibrations.

NICE TRICKS
do no evil

While medieval hermetics jealously guarded their sacred secret "As above, so below," some must have wondered whether it extended to "as within, so without." Later, Freud and Jung suggested that perceptions are largely projections, and things that make you feel angry are caused either by your denial of them within yourself or to yourself, or they trigger a past trauma or a toddler tantrum (thwarted in attaining a goal).

In Eastern cultures, losing emotional control is considered a loss of face. So to keep a smile whatever the provocation, accept that you have personally created the present circumstance, and whatever the other person is doing, they are serving you.

Try going out of your way to do something nice (or nasty) for another person, and notice their response, and how you feel. In Aristotle's *Ethics*, he recommends walking a middle way between an excess and a deficiency of the virtues; for example, courage is the mean between rashness and cowardice, and generosity is the mean between wastefulness and stinginess (*see also opposite*).

In the ancient Egyptian code of Ma'at, 42 affirmations were made at the end of a day or a life, e.g., "I have not killed," "I have not caused offence," or "I have not polluted the water." Moses later turned these into Thou Shalt Nots, but the difference in personal responsibility is huge. Try the older version!

 Complete acceptance includes recognizing and accepting one's own non-acceptance. Ask yourself "What am I doing or not doing that enables the other person to be this way?"

Simply treat others as you would like to be treated yourself.

Above: Rich Mr. Thin shows aloof disdain for the poor Scruffy family. They think he's an arrogant prig.

Above: Angry Mr. Fussy shows his deep sense of gratitude for yet another beautifully served dinner.

Above: Idle Mr. Serfcrusher projects his own laziness on to honest Bob, who had just finished a hard day's labor.

Above: Crass Mr. Deville shows his unusual sensitivity to animal welfare on his way back from the park.

Quick-Fix Tricks
a useful toolkit

A stitch in time saves nine, and quick fixes have been used for thousands of years, whether mending the grass roof, or, like Caesar, rapidly adapting a battle plan to fit changing circumstances.

Complaints can be annoying. Tradesmen for centuries have dealt with them by simply staying calm, quiet, with an open body stance, good eye contact, and making notes while smiling. Medieval donkey traders probably imagined complaints splatting on the barn wall behind them. Ancient Greeks offered gifts to the Gods, to placate the difficult spirit assumed to have taken over the person, enabling both parties to blame something else for the incident, a great trick for recovering a strained relationship.

Quick fixes, while not addressing the deeper issues, nevertheless resolve many of life's problems and keep things moving. Changing clothes, *reorganizing* the layout or furnishing of a room, working in unusual places or taking some exercise all provide the context for innovative thinking and behavior. Moving to some different spaces can create fresh perspectives, allowing new insights to emerge.

If you experience an unpleasant emotion, notice where you feel it in your body. Ask yourself what might be inside the emotion. And what might be inside that? After several layers most people will arrive at a sense of inner peace or love. This is the default human condition, into which quick fixes can offer brief glimpses.

Above: Think of a problem. Notice where your eyes focus and what you imagine at that location. Turn around full circle and notice any difference. Repeat six times.

Above: Vectors. Strange though it may seem, memories are related to precise directions and distances in eye focus. A sphere of precise memories surrounds every one of us. For example, if a large spider scared you as a baby and it was up and to the left of you, then it will still be there. If today you imagine a scary spider, your eyes will again flick up and to the left. So, using this, think of a problem. Notice where your eyes go, and what might be there. You can now replace it with something pleasureable (a swish), use the spin (left), or any number of other quick fixes.

Above: A squash. Two conflicting or opposing beliefs, behaviors, or desires? Try this trick. Place one in each hand. In turn visualize and feel them until solid. Find their common higher purpose. Let them merge and bring your hands to your chest.

Left: A simple timeline trick. Identify a problem from your past. Notice where your past, present and future are, as a line on the floor. Notice the context and positive intentions of those involved. What resources might you have needed then? Step on to the line at the present point (1, opposite) and follow the sequence, gifting your younger self the resources at (3).

SYSTEMS SPELLS
changing parts to change the whole

Some fixes make things worse. Hercules cut off one of the Hydra's heads only to watch two more grow in its place. Applying a systems thinking trick he burned the stumps, thus finishing the labor.

Systems are self-contained networks, living or otherwise, exisiting within a context. Systems self-organize, generating unpredictable properties. If a system starts to produce undesirable behavior, then its structure normally needs to change. To find the best place to intervene ask "why is this happening?" and list any answers in a row. Under each answer, ask "why" again, continuing the process until patterns and sources begin to emerge. Factors can be joined by arrows showing cycles or cause-effect links (*opposite top*).

Zoom in to some typical examples of systems thinking (*below*).

Today's Problems come from yesterday's solutions

Clean up crime in one district, it will increase in another. In a complex system, cause and effect are seldom close because of the many intervening parts and delays, yet people usually assume the opposite.

The Harder you Push, the harder the System pushes back

The more hours you work, the less effective you become. Attempting superfast growth, or massive short-term gain is seldom the winning move as it stresses other parts of the system

Small Changes can produce Big Results

This is because the areas of highest leverage are seldom obvious. When turning an oil tanker round, moving the rudder is too hard. Instead the rudder has a tiny rudder, called a trim tab, which is used to turn the main rudder.

The Easy Way Out usually leads back in

Low leverage interventions often appear to work in the short term. Give a man a fish and he will eat, give a man a book and he will feed himself. Give a man a trawler and his grandchildren might not end up with any fish (see opposite)

The Cure can be worse than the Disease

Sometimes the easy solution is not just ineffective, it can be addictive or dangerous. Government interventions can foster dependency. Any supposed help that weakens the host system should be suspect.

Have your Cake and Eat It but not at the same time

To have bigger quality and lower costs, focus on quality systems first. Dividing an elephant in half does not produce two small elephants. Think of whole systems. Beware slow changes which cook frogs gently.

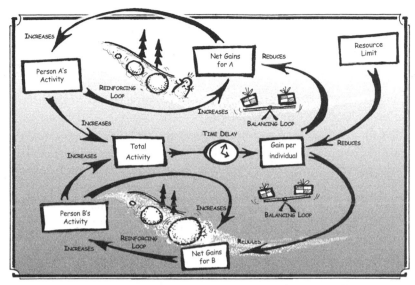

Above. The Tragedy of the Commons. Individuals use a limited resource available to all in common, e.g., fish. At first it is easy to get the resource, but as more people use it, they each get less. They intensify their efforts, accelerating the depletion. The fish in the ocean have nearly all gone. The solution is either a strong moderating authority, or a partitioning of the resource.

Above: A vicious circle turns into a virtuous circle. Both are reinforcing loops. On the left Urg criticizes Mona's new dress, making her upset, so she responds by making it a bone of contention. Their life becomes a misery. On the right Urg tells Mona how beautiful she looks. She glows, becoming even more attractive, and admires his bone. Happy ever after!

MOVING THE GOALPOSTS
tricks of the as yet unthought of

Whatever you think you want, something different always emerges. Alexander the Great was famous for moving the goal posts; he cut the Gordian knot to fulfil the prophecy that whoever undid it would rule the world; he treated his Persian subjects equally to his Macedonians; he even took his army into India, which was beyond the then known world, and he changed the rules of warfare. The trick is to think differently; if you are not winning then change the rules! Some governments do this whenever it suits them.

Strangely, the opposite of what people want often works better for them. Desires only exist because of a lack. Eliminate the lack and that old desire should look after itself. For example, wanting better safety, schools can often add rules which actually stop children from learning how to play safely. Another trick involves defining what you want and asking yourself how you would know you had it. Often this evidence of knowing turns out to be the real object of desire and, in most instances it is also much easier to achieve.

The following step-by-step trick deconstructs limiting world views and replaces them with something new. Choose a project you want to enhance. Begin by defining it in some detail, then place your scribblings somewhere and step back. Now, in stages, study your perceptions of the project so far; ask yourself what knowledge is embodied in projects of this kind; explore the world around the edges and discover the external factors that might have some bearing; think back through the steps that have led you to where you are now; pause, reflect, and re-express your vision; work out a new detailed plan of action. Try it for yourself!

Above: David moves the goalposts and redefines the nature of the battle to defeat Goliath.

SLIPPING PAST THE GUARDS
and other attention spells

Guards come in many guises—dragons watch over treasure, police serve a state—but many are invisible, supporting the familiar patterns of the ego, preventing self-realization. Getting past these guards involves a multitude of tricks, some as old as time itself.

The *sugar-coated pill* is a good example of a trick that enables the delivery of an otherwise unacceptable weapon. The Trojan Horse, or wolf in sheep's clothing, are other examples. They work because we normally judge things by their surface appearance.

Pickpockets and conjurors use distractions to focus their clients' attention on a specific target thus reducing their awareness elsewhere, while they ply their trade. This is why guarding is close to a meditative state when done properly—a guard holds no focus, but maintains all-around sensing. Politicians use distractions, burying bad news in the middle of a period of sensational news, getting past the press. Just as hypnosis is all about managing the focus of awareness, so too are trickster's spells, so if you feel blown off course, wonder about the motives of those around you!

Attention, while it can be directed, also exists as a sensitive sphere around you. Most people know when they are being stared at, so learn to look to one side of people you don't want to notice you. Perseus had to use a mirrored shield to get close to super-psychic Medusa. To develop your sensitivity, have a friend hold up a dollar bill between your fingers and release it. Try and catch it. Hard, eh? Now try with your eyes closed. For most people it turns out this is much easier, because the eyes deceive, and it is more accurate to rely upon your feelings, once they are trained and trusted.

Above: Dodger suddenly spots a beautiful bird in a high window, enabling Fingers to run off with the goods.

Above: Dodger yawns to project sleepiness onto Private Sharp, and waits for him to fall asleep before stealing his lunch.

Above: When creeping up on a guard, never look at the body. Private Sharp will sense being stared at.

Above: Much better. This time Dodger meekly places his attention to the side, and wins some lunch.

Above: Dodger navigates the attention-field of Private Sharp to avoid the especially sensitive spots.

Above: Dodger controls the vibe, effectively making Fats invisible to the crowd and guard.

FLEXIBILITY TRICKS
bending in the wind

For thousands of years Indian Yogis have shown that flexible bodies are good for you, but flexible minds may be better still, because it is the mind that instructs the body to hold pain or stiffness or lack of flexibility (unconscious bodies are much more bendy).

Equally ancient, Eastern martial arts teach muscle memory, installing patterns of movement that work without thought, a trick used by top sports players today. In Tai-chi the body takes over the movements entirely, allowing a volition-free experience. Japanese Taiko drumming is likewise based upon giving up conscious control of the body, this time to the spirit of the drum.

How flexible are you? Try touching your toes, hang from a branch, sing from below your deepest note to above your highest, practice crawling like a baby, laugh at a joke which offended you, give up eating meat, or if you did already then eat a steak, make fun of your problems, listen carefully for all the everyday sounds you normally miss, watch the saddest film ever followed by the silliest.

The original cause of a present behavior exists as a memory because long ago it interrupted the smooth flow of project-and-perceive awareness. The original attractor might have been as simple as a stubbed toe (*lower opposite*), which then attracted further reinforcing events and a compensating behavior, overlaying the original until effective compensation for all of these events developed. Go within the layers (*see page 11*) to find the causes and patterns. The attractor is undone by returning and reconnecting bodily to the awareness prior to the original event. The present self can then expand and live without the compensation.

Above: Ariki, not a chip off the old block, and thoroughly bored of fixed designs in her society, decides to show off some new directions in art, seeking to encourage greater flexibility in the aesthetic perceptions of her fellow islanders.

Above: Jokes worldwide enable emotional release, greater flexibility of mind, and refreshing perspectives.

Above: Dancing round the fire. A flexible body reflects and helps to develop a flexible mind, lighting the embers of change.

Above: Trog wonders why he feels so heavy-footed. Working back in time he remembers he's often had cuts and bruises on his right foot. Going back further he remembers the first time he stubbed his toe. Releasing the memory breaks his cycle.

33

GOING WITH THE FLOW
tricks that make life easier

When Hercules was asked to clean the massive and filthy Augean Stables in a single day, instead of doing the job as expected, he found an easier solution, diverting two local rivers through the buildings. A few thousand years later, in Sir Isaac Newton's time, physicists discovered a related principle, *The Path of Least Resistance*. If something is a struggle, then try another way. Sometimes it pays to work with the symptoms, not to fight them.

Flow can be developed in body, emotions, mind, and spirit. For instance, from sitting, lean your head forward (almost down) and a pendulum effect will bring your whole body up to standing, effortlessly! In the morning, roll out of bed, placing both feet on the ground simultaneously, and your momentum will spring you up. How else can you work with your body structure?

Emotional flow comes from allowing passion in the body. A dissociated person sees or hears the emotions of others, while associated people feel them. It is the fear of perceived pain that stops people associating. If your flow is blocked, ask your fear what its purpose is, and what that achieves. In what different ways might you achieve your goal? Which way feels best? Make sure you agree with all of your being and that no part of you objects.

Mental flow is constrained by internal dialogue. To reduce this, ask each voice why it's there, and help it to do its job differently (every part of you is only trying to help!). Keep on doing this until you have no more thoughts! Or practice Vipassana meditation, focusing attention entirely on your breath, one of India's most ancient mind tricks, rediscovered by Gautama Buddha over 2500 years ago.

Above: Spiritual flow. To align himself with his highest purpose in life Tonto goes on a vision quest. Alone in the wilderness, he fasts for days, meditates, and drinks some pokey local plant extracts before receiving a visitation from the spirit world. Finally the ancestors give him a vision of his life's journey and his new name Smiling Bull.

Above: The River of Life. Huang-Li is under the illusion that he controls his destiny, but the river of life actually offers just a few key decision points for him to travel down different channels for certain lengths of time before entering the sea.

ZEST TRICKS
increasing your energy

The central doctrine of Buddhist practice is the Eightfold Path, a useful box of tricks involving right understanding, resolve, speech, conduct, livelihood, effort, mindfulness, and meditation. So, by first knowing your resolve, you can then choose your perfect livelihood and other aligned ways of being. Because this minimizes resistance, it also minimizes down time, and limitless enthusiasm and energy emerge. The path can also serve as a powerful business tool. Try it!

Deep within us all is an indomitable rock of inner strength that, once accessed, bestows invulnerability. To find this secret space, seek deep within the solar plexus/sacral area, named the *hara* by the ancient Japanese. A related trick is to recall a time when you felt unbeatable, winning a game, or knowing something with such total confidence that nothing could touch you.

Putting any dependence on something external, for instance, a "performance-enhancing" drug, associates life-force out of the body, reducing overall zest. Like body, like mind. A simple trick is to get the body going early in the day, generating momentum and energy for a good day's thinking. Go for a morning jog, or try *Tai Chi*, practiced for thousands of years by the Chinese, which teaches the art of flowing with the body's movements, and where, for example, a raising arm lifts itself and stays up without effort.

Charisma is a kind of zesty magnetism projected through the eyes and body. To boost your charisma practice loving yourself and loving those around you. Assume that everyone is acting through love, and discover the true nature of others and yourself. The more you love your neighbor the more your charisma grows.

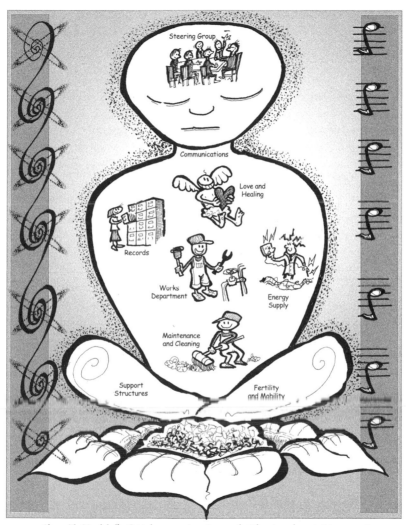

Above: The Numbskulls. Get to know your inner team, and set them to work maximizing your zest. Talk to them, listen to them, organize them into projects, and give them control over what they do best.

37

MIND CONTROL
cockpit and dashboard tricks

If Herod had only had a little more control over his faculties he might have escaped being so entranced by Salome's dancing, and John the Baptist might have kept his head. The opposite of pure flow is absolute control. In engineering, control is what moderates flow, like taps on water pipes. For the mind, control leads to progressive release, as long as the control is directive not suppressive.

Modern mind-control tricks involve visualizations of control systems (*lower opposite*). Imagine, visualize, feel, and hear a meter with a dial, representing some function of your system. Point at the current setting, and then wobble it to experience moving the energy level. To leverage the effect, now visualize a ratchet control for your belief in the energy level meter, and use the same process to raise this. Do the same for the belief in the belief, and so on.

Recurring thoughts are messages that need to be addressed. Express them positively and ask your subconscious to work on them. Another trick to address a chattering mind is to write down everything that comes into it. Cut out and group together statements with similar handwriting or themes. Find out more about these parts of your personal collective. The chattering mind just wants your attention, like a group of noisy children (*below*). Assure them they will each have their turn and order them in line!

Above: Many religions, traditions, and philosophies have practices that encourage control of mind, body, and emotion, whether visualizing, praying, chanting mantras, meditating or working the body.

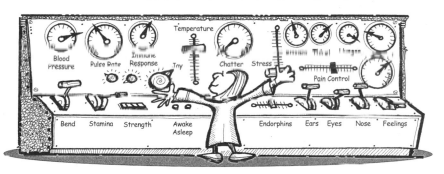

Above: Maxwell visualizes and sets the body controls for various parameters of his state, making sure he is happy and stress-free. By practicing this mind trick regularly, you can even make white skin develop melatonin.

RELEASING SPELLS
freeing the prisoners of the mind

One of the oldest tricks for many ills known worldwide is to tie a knot while thinking of a problem, and bury it. As the knot rots so the energy in the problem is released. Other ancient releasing spells involve cutting symbolic cords, purification by fire or water, and rites of passage. Laughter too, through comedy and satire, has supplied relief that has mostly kept politicians safe from the masses for eons.

Other techniques are more modern. The Fast Phobia Cure (*opposite top*) takes 10-20 minutes to scramble the access of the fear. Another trick involves grabbing the focus of attention of the person with the fear (*middle opposite*). This can resolve fears in seconds, even if more than one vectored location (*see page 25*) has to be grabbed and moved. If someone has total belief in you, just create an expectation of healing and their fear will clear instantly.

Another fast way to release stuck pains, feelings, or thoughts is to start describing them through "ings." For example "feeling paining legging footing ankling spreading shifting hurting ouching aarggh-ing phewing breathing relaxing releasing going calming fading nothing." Though it may sound strange to people around you, it works by making the experience present and ongoing so that the mind has to let go and the symptoms flow away.

Another releasing trick used for millennia is dramatic re-enactment. Examples come from grief-relieving plays in a necropolis to dream therapy, which works by reliving a dream from the point of view of each actor. Other forms have people enact the roles of significant characters, under the direction of the central character, who then experiences the drama emerging (*lower, opposite*).

Above: The Fast Phobia Cure. Antonius, terrified of snakes, watches himself nervously watching a video of his younger self being terrorized by a large serpent. Changing the color, contrast and quality of the picture transforms fear into laughter.

Above: The five-second vectored smash-and-grab phobia cure. Livia notices Caesar focusing on an imaginary scary spider, so she grabs it while he's still focused on the scary spot and removes it. Optionally she can paste something nice in its place.

Above: Psychodramatic release. Antonius, still terrified by snakes, directs a dramatic re-enactment of the story of his terror of large serpents, no longer recoiling in horror. Members of the audience witness the events and empathize with him.

RESCALING
a trick that unravels larger knots

Long-term patterns, addictions, bad habits, and major illnesses rarely have quick fixes but require a deeper process for healing. The purpose is to attain either complete remission or acceptance.

One of the ultimate goals of Zen Buddhism [700 AD] is to be at one with the world, and the purpose of rescaling is to attain this in relation to a serious problem, moving into 1-to-1 scale with the world, seeing things as they are. It is also the condition for awakening enlightenment, or full embodiment of spirit.

This trick often works best with a friend, one of you guiding the other. The person with the problem starts scaled far out of proportion to the issue, as if seeing it through a telescope or microscope, and makes a drawing of what they see. Zooming out, they make a new drawing of the factors around the original. Progressively zooming out and making new drawings brings them to the same scale as the problem, looking out through their own eyes in a younger self that was present just before the moment that was the source of the problem. This reconnects the frozen part of the younger self back to the here and now, effecting a rapid growing up that sometimes may take a few days to integrate.

Scaling can be applied to any drawings, words, gestures, movements, nonverbal sounds, and feelings that a person might have. Ask your friend simple questions like "and does anything else go on there?", "and what could be just around that?", or "and what could be over there?" Your job is to bring their attention to spaces, actions, or words that are adjacent to, but just outside, their present focus of attention. It's easier than it sounds!

Above: Example 1. Kate feels flat, and out of touch with herself. "I am not into Kate!" she says. She starts by writing "KATE," then doodles around. As she zooms out, she discovers that Kate is in an eye, and zooming further, that it is the eye of a dinosaur, who is then found on a plain during a meteor strike. It is the KT extinction. She remembers she was once Katie, and was watching a program about this. She is now at one with her true name and has her 'I' back.

Above: Example 2. Matthew lacks trust. He begins by writing "Trust" and as a joke writes "trussed" too. Zooming out he makes a new picture with more words around, finding some opposites. He recalls a time at school learning about opposites. Zooming out he draws the school and the stream alongside it. Moving away, the stream becomes a snake, and he suddenly recalls watching Jungle Book and the scene with Mowgli and Ka shown above, releasing his mistrust.

43

Inside-Out Tricks
turning the world back to front

In *Exodus*, it is said that the sins of the fathers shall be punished to the third and fourth generations. An eye for an eye, a tooth for a tooth, is the old way. Indeed, many people blame their parents, schooling, or upbringing for some of the problems that they later face in life. Powerful tricks can help with this mind set.

Some Eastern traditions highlight truth and blame and encourage seeing the world inverted from conventional reality. The wise Sufi fool Mulla Nasruddin perceives the world inside out, back to front and upside down. Prey attracts its predator. Instead of being born in sin everyone can be considered perfect as they are. There are no acts of hate, only acts of love. Turning the world on its head can bring new perspectives. In the normal world, people unwittingly project onto others and blame them for reflecting their own imperfections, whereas in reality we can only see ourselves in others.

In the example opposite, a series of truth questions explores the chain of cause and effect, blame and source, which ultimately leads to the destruction of an unhelpful world view. These questions require you to work with a friend and are most effective if the questioner asks them detached from any agenda of their own.

"Forgive them Father, for they know not what they do," said Jesus, breaking with the old way. Forgiveness is an excellent way to invert judgment into acceptance of the other. Imagine a stage. In turn, call onto it your parents, siblings, grandparents, friends, colleagues, bosses, customers, suppliers, teachers, celebrities, races, religions, and so on. Thank each in turn. Forgive each one, ask and receive their forgiveness, and remember their unique message.

44

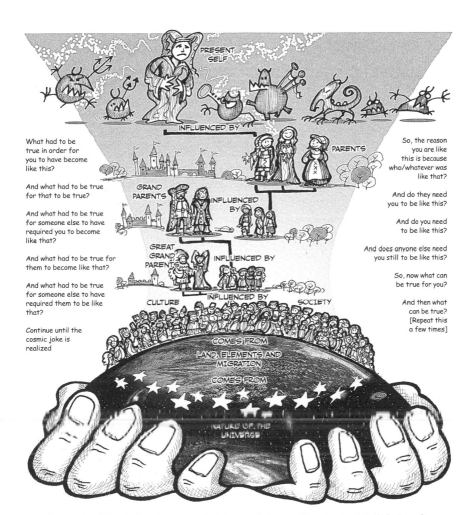

Above: Contessa Sofia seeks the truth of her woes. Following the path of truth and blame, by asking "what had to be true" in order for each stage of her journey to have become true (left side), she finds that first her parents, then her grandparents, then her great grandparents and so on, had all required the next to become a certain way. Ultimately she realizes her woes are an accidental consequence of the nature of the universe. She now builds a new truth tree, devoid of woes (right side).

MIND OVER ENZYME
tricks which change everything about you

Early proto-religions, Egyptian, Oceanic, Native American, and later Celtic were animistic, worshipping and celebrating the spiritual powers of animals. They honored the diversity of life on Earth, working with it, rather than against it.

Allergies are on the increase throughout the modern world and largely result from the body-mind opposing nature in some form, whether the pollen of flowers, bee-stings, or seeds (wheat or nuts). Many of the tricks already presented in this book can alleviate or eliminate such allergies. For instance, strange though it may seem, why not make a deal with the "Great Spirit" of the mosquitos (*opposite*), subtly changing your body chemistry, much like changing diet by ceasing eating dairy, meat, wheat, or sweets. Reducing your fear of being bitten will even change your smell.

Simple tricks also make a difference. Take time to love your food and utensils before preparation and eating to make peace with your dinner! Check the food you buy for good vibes, and thank it before you eat it. Sleep well, wash with fewer chemicals, stretch, keep fit and eat well to keep a healthy body chemistry (*below*). It's all common sense. Or try fasting—after the body has had no food for five days it begins to devour fat, release toxins and weaken cancers.

Enzymes in your body turn your genes on or off. Imagine being able to do this consciously. Ultimately, the body is the mind.

Above: Zoe can't eat wheat. She asks her body why it reacts and remembers being overfed bread as a child. She releases her early body memory using a trick in this book (e.g., page 11), and tucks into a yummy sandwich.

47

SELF-DEFENSE TRICKS
or how to deal with bullies

No one likes being bullied. And being shown up in front of your friends isn't nice either. Socrates would take an opening statement that was true on the surface and then, through an irrefutable chain of logic, lead his victim to agree that they were wrong (the Socratic Method). The Athenians poisoned him with hemlock!

Bullies are frightened of bigger bullies, and evil likes to present a polished appearance. Bullying is based upon secrecy and lies, hoping the victim will not tell. So begin by telling those authority figures the bully is most afraid of (not always obvious). The bully's fears engage and their behavior desists. Or invite them to play.

Manipulation is slightly different. If someone is trying to put one over on you, they will probably fish for an initial "yes" from you with an opening gambit like: "Let me put to you," "I invite you to," "I put to you, that," "Would you accept that," "Trust me," "Maybe you caused," "With respect," "Are you with me?," "Thanks for agreeing to listen," "Would you give me the power to," "As a friend." Early signs of manipulation include feeling confused, wrong, shame, or fault. Defend by politely declining, or return the compliment, "I invite you to leave me alone."

The bullying game often has a pattern (*below*). An easy intervention is to decline the rescue, robbing the bully of the payoff.

Above: Hierarchy vs Heterarchy. Defend against pyramidal power structures by forming tribal circles.

Above: Manipulation vs Cooperation. Defend against grim string pullers by working as a team.

Above: Divide-and-Rule vs Freedom-n-Love. Defend against compartmentalization by playing together.

Above: Dictatorship vs Democracy. Defend against an evil dictator by mobilizing the people in passive resistance.

DEFENSE AGAINST DARK ARTS
dealing with projection and manipulation

Across the world, in almost every culture and age, there are stories of fairies, elves, djinn, dæmons, and other entities who lend their powers to mankind for the weaving of magical spells and incantations, for good and ill purposes. True or not, many people sometimes experience what they can only describe as "dark forces" in their lives, and a few tricks up your sleeve can be very useful.

In Japan, a business card will be held, regarded and retained a few times. Only if the energy feels right does business proceed. This is a form of psychic defense, for some slippery characters may give you a gift just to create a way into your life. To cleanse an object, place a crystal on it, wash it or leave it in a stream for a day, hold and send love to it, bury it for a few days, run a counter-projection spell (*page 17*), or just throw it away.

If you feel drained by a person, ask yourself about their behavior and how they use their words. If they use "you" a lot they might be projecting their own issues onto you, and resisting projections can burn a lot of energy. Use the mind tricks shown (*opposite*) to defend yourself against shady characters who exploit your weak spots, crawl uninvited into your personal space, or leech off your energy.

A good trick for disentangling yourself from someone is to imagine a blue-gold bubble or ribbon around the two of you, and then pinch or twist it until it divides into two separate spaces (*below*).

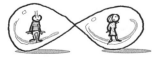

Above: The Lightning Rod. Conduct negative projections, dark thoughts, headaches, etc into the earth.

Above: The Golden (sometimes Silver) Bubble. Protect yourself from harm inside a sphere of love.

Above: Bottling the Genie. Place a bubble of love around the evildoer, only allowing good vibes through.

Above: Balance. The gremlin is an aspect of yourself. Be lighthearted and use their own heaviness against them.

Above: Advertising uses the dark arts by attaching commercial objects to your triggered emotions. Stay alert!

THE SHAMAN'S CLOAK
tricks to access other worlds

Tradition has it that on All Hallows Eve, the old Celtic New Year, the veils thin and the spirits of the ancestors bring messages to the living. Many tribal cultures imagine the earth as a playground of incarnate beings, watched over and served by hosts of metaphysical beings.

To visit the underworld, like Odysseus visiting Hades, first ask for an appropriate guide by thinking, asking aloud, or, like some shamans, employing animal spirits, plants or minerals. Summon an archetypal figure, like Gabriel, Wotan, Triton, or Merlin by calling their name. Make a portal between worlds using your divine pet cat or the world tree in your garden. Or choose a plant or animal, picture it, start to move and makes noises like it. Become it, look out through its eyes, and ask what it knows. Use your childlike imagination to open your eyes and ears to this new world, and watch what happens.

Shamanism works by collapsing the veils between the worlds, and by allowing things in one world to stand for things in another (*see also page 8*). A shaken rattle becomes the sound of rain, encouraging the same, and magical objects act as powerful anchors in the shaman's psyche. A column of light and dark built by a shaman can help earthbound spirits to pass on, clearing spooky houses.

Plants and animals are part of the conscious continuum, just like humans. Talk to your plants and they will respond. Love life around you and it will glow with happiness. We too are loved and supported by unseen forces. Perhaps airplanes fly because angels uphold the laws of physics and mathematics!

EARTH MAGIC
tricks that make things happen

In Japan, the spirits in living nature are called *kami*, while the Native American Algonquian people know them as *Manitou*. Traditional earth magic relies on working with spirits and subtle telluric currents to create changes in the world's everyday causal matrix. Hawaiian Kahuna sorcerers claim to be able to do anything from healing, cursing, or blessing, to playing with elementals (powers of earth, air, wind, and water). The Kahuna use a spirit called an *avaiku* to, for example, bring fish to bait.

There are many ways to call for a storm or a rainbow. You may want to wield the energy yourself, or instead engage the air spirits and ask them to stir things up. Another way might be to address the world within your mind and look for an external parallel, or plug into the earth's neural network of ley lines and send a request.

Learning to sense subtle energies like ley lines is much easier than you might think. Start by discovering the aura of energy around a person, by bouncing your hands off it. Or take up dowsing and experience for yourself the strange feeling you get on discovering the path of a buried water pipe. Or use two hands to find out how to balance *chakras* (seven energy centers running up the body) for a friend. Experiment with making magical objects like wands, or staffs, using wood and crystals. Which ones sing for you?

Earth magic can boost your love life too. Tune in to the relevant zones of your and your partner's bodies and visualize and feel potent energies cycling and building between you. Or warm them up on a cold night by tuning in to their solar plexus and turning its volume up. Remember the earth is alive and you are part of it.

Above: Drew chooses a good place for a temple, with the right geometry of hills and water, Sun, & Moon.

Above: Drew's first successful attempt at befriending Aeolus, the ruler of the winds.

Above: Drew goes on a pilgrimage to the natural spring source of his local river.

Above: Drew studies the motions of the heavenly bodies, their influence on Earth, and how to build in tune.

QUANTUM TRICKERY
developing a new kind of mind

It is roughly one hundred years since relativity and quantum mechanics were first proposed to a skeptical scientific community, and yet very few people walking around today have any idea that the world they see is made of virtual particles, behaving in utterly strange and magical ways, or that time itself changes depending on how fast you are travelling.

These quantum laws are known to apply from the microscopic to the cosmological scale, so they apply to you and me! "In the beginning" could well be a misperception; maybe time goes backwards and forwards from now. Realizing the consciousness of every single particle and the entire cosmos, the new wizards will be those who can think equations alive, manipulating matter, space and time through pure thought.

Over 300 years ago Natural Philosophy split into science (the physically observable universe), and philosophy (the metaphysical). It is time to heal that rift, and consider consciousness, mind and matter as parts of a whole that can only be understood as one.

Whether you want to read minds, see auras or become an instant method actor, the tools are in this book—and they work. If not, ask "how come I cannot do this, yet others can?" and use some of the other tricks to address the answers! The tricks have been used for eons, they are here modernized and scientific, predictable, repeatable and observable in the mind's eye.

As the ancients knew well, "All is Mind," for the world is illusion, and seeing through the Emperor's new clothes leads to joys and worlds beyond the wildest dreams. Enjoy the now; it is all there is.

Above: The hills are alive. Every rock, plant, animal and cloud has a unique animating spirit, its soul. Open your eyes, ears, mind, and subtle senses to walk in another world, parallel to normal human reality.

Above: Bilocation. Concentrate the frequency of your wavepacket, spreading it in space, lowering the frequency where an astral projection is desired.

Above: Applying bilocation to telekinesis. A version of yourself is projected and invisibly picks up a teacup. Alternatively employ a poltergeist - much easier!

Appendix - Freudian Defenses

Defense mechanisms are psychological devices used by individuals to cope with the world and maintain and protect the self-image. It can be a useful exercise to try and identify those which you think you employ. Next ask a friend to indentify the ones which he/she thinks you employ. Are they the same ones?

Compensating: *behaving in a new way because one cannot accomplish another way.*

Denying: *unconsciously resolving emotional conflict and reducing anxiety by refusing to perceive the more unpleasant aspects of external reality.*

Denying awareness: *avoiding pain and harm by stating one was in a different state of awareness (e.g. alcohol/drug intoxication) or psychological state (e.g. mad).*

Denying cycle: *avoiding looking at one's decisions leading up to an event or not considering one's pattern of decision making and how harmful behavior is repeating.*

Denying denying: *thinking, acting and behaving for bolstering confidence that nothing needs changing in one's personal behaving.*

Denying fact: *typically lying in order to avoid facts that one thinks may be potentially painful to oneself or to others.*

Denying impact: *avoiding thinking about or understanding the harms one's behavior has caused to oneself or to others. By doing this, one may avoid feeling guilty. This may be preventing one from developing remorse or empathizing with others.*

Denying responsibility: *usually attempting to avoid potential harm or pain by shifting attention away from oneself.*

Dissociating: *separating or postponing a feeling that normally would accompany a situation or thought.*

Displacing: *unconsciously, mind redirecting emotion from a "dangerous" object to a "safe" object. For example, punching cushions when angry at another person.*

Humor (Joking): *refocusing attention on the somewhat comical side of the situation to relieve negative tension; similar to comic relief.*

Idealizing: *presenting the object of attention as "all good," masking true negative feelings toward the other (person).*

Identifying: *unconsciously modelling one's self upon another person's behavior.*

Introjecting: *identifying with some idea or object so deeply that it becomes a part of that person.*

Inverting: *refocusing aggression or emotions evoked from an external force onto one's self.*

Intellectualizing: *concentrating on the intellectual components of situations for distancing oneself from the anxiety-provoking emotions associated with these situations.*

Projecting: *attributing to others one's own unacceptable or unwanted thoughts and/or emotions. Projection reduces anxiety by allowing the expression of the impulse or desire without letting the ego recognize it.*

Rationalizing: *constructing a logical justification for a decision that was originally made through a different mental process.*

Reaction forming: *converting into their opposites unconscious wishes or impulses that are perceived to be dangerous.*

Regressing: *reverting to an earlier stage of development in the face of unacceptable impulses.*

Repressing: *pushing thoughts into the unconscious and preventing painful or dangerous thoughts from entering consciousness.*

Somatizing: *manifesting emotional anxiety through physical symptoms.*

Splitting: *seeing external objects or people as either "all good" or "all bad."*

Sublimating: *refocusing psychic energy away from negative outlets to more positive outlets. Drives which cannot find an outlet are re-channeled.*

Substituting: *replacing one feeling or emotion with another.*

Suppressing: *consciously pushing thoughts into the preconscious.*

Undoing: *trying to 'undo' negative or threatening thoughts by one's actions.*